TI0620989

WITHDRAWN

Foods of Egypt

Barbara Sheen

KIDHAVEN PRESS
A part of Gale, Cengage Learning

Detroit • New York • San Francisco • New Haven, Conn • Waterville, Maine • London

GALE
CENGAGE Learning™

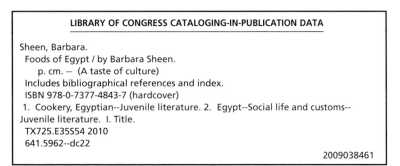

LIBRARY OF CONGRESS CATALOGING-IN-PUBLICATION DATA

Sheen, Barbara.
  Foods of Egypt / by Barbara Sheen.
    p. cm. -- (A taste of culture)
  Includes bibliographical references and index.
  ISBN 978-0-7377-4843-7 (hardcover)
  1. Cookery, Egyptian--Juvenile literature. 2. Egypt--Social life and customs--Juvenile literature. I. Title.
  TX725.E35S54 2010
  641.5962--dc22

                                                    2009038461

Kidhaven Press
27500 Drake Rd.
Farmington Hills MI 48331

ISBN-13: 978-0-7377-4843-7
ISBN-10: 0-7377-4843-5

Printed in the United States of America
1 2 3 4 5 6 7 14 13 12 11 10

Printed by Bang Printing, Brainerd, MN, 1st Ptg., 04/2010

Contents

Ancient Ingredients

Egyptian civilization is more than five thousand years old. The past is always nearby in this ancient land. Pyramids and other monuments dot the landscape. The food Egyptians eat also reflects the nation's long history. Modern Egyptian meals contain much the same ingredients as those eaten in the time of the pharaohs.

Although most of Egypt is desert where little grows, for as long as Egyptians can remember, the rich soil of the Nile Valley has supported 99 percent of the population on the nation's only cultivable land. It has provided Egyptians with an abundance of different foods such as dates, grapes, artichokes, onions, leeks, pomegranates,

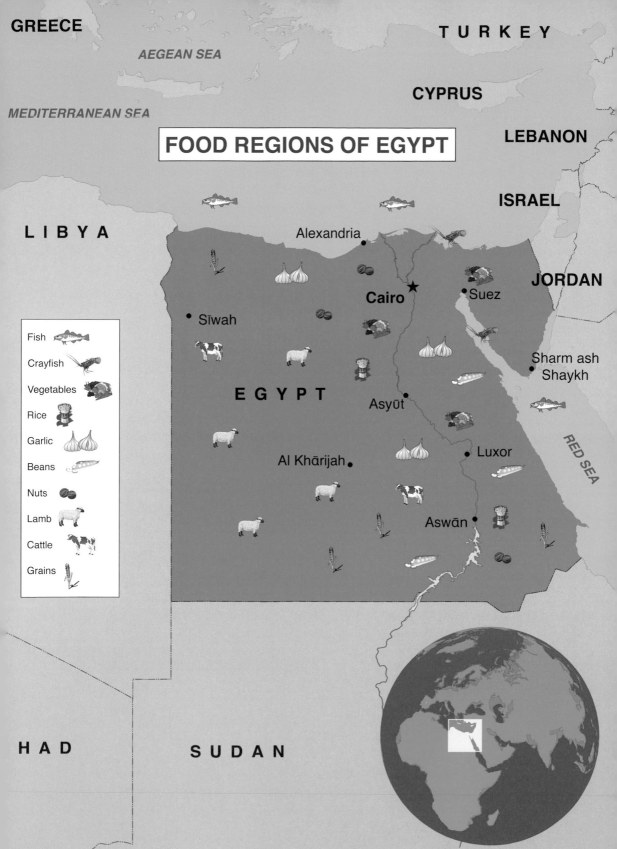

FOOD REGIONS OF EGYPT

The Nile River

The Nile River is the longest river in the world. It flows south to north for 4,150 miles (6,679km) through much of Africa. Egypt is its most northern part.

In ancient times, during the summer the Nile flooded, spreading over nearby valleys. When the floodwaters subsided, they left rich soil behind. This provided the ancient Egyptians with fertile land in which almost anything grew. Egyptian farmers planted crops in November and harvested them in April. The soil was so rich that they often replanted after spring harvest and gathered another crop before the Nile flooded again. Today the Aswan Dam regulates the Nile River's flow.

The floodwaters of the Nile River leave behind fertile soil, which Egyptian farmers use to plant a variety of crops.

figs, nuts, olives, garlic, greens, eggplants, and radishes. The Mediterranean Sea and the waters of the Nile River have given them fish. And, although grazing land is scarce, cattle, sheep, and goats have been raised here for centuries, as have rabbits, chickens, and pigeons. For thousands of years, all of these foods have been a part of the Egyptian diet. But it is wheat, legumes, and spices that Egyptian cooks have always depended on.

Ancient Loaves

Wheat has played a key role in Egyptian life since ancient times. Ancient Egyptians were the first people to understand the leavening process. That is, the process of using yeast or a souring agent to make bread rise. Once early Egyptians discovered the leavening process, they began baking bread, which became the mainstay of their diet. It provided them with protein, carbohydrates, and minerals. Everyone, from slaves to pharaohs, ate bread at every meal. In fact, they mass produced bread to feed to slaves and workers constructing the pyramids and other government projects.

Bread was so important to ancient Egyptians that they decorated ancient tombs with wall paintings depicting the bread-making process, from the planting of wheat to the baking of bread. The Egyptians also put bread loaves inside tombs to ensure that the dead would not go hungry in the next world. They shaped bread dough into animal and human figures so that the dead would have companions in the next world. Archaeologists have found a number of five-thousand-year-old bread loaves, which are perfectly preserved due to Egypt's dry climate.

The Staff of Life

Bread is still a vital part of the Egyptian diet. No meal is considered complete without it. Indeed, bread is so important to Egyptians that **aish** (esh), the Egyptian word for bread means "life."

Egyptians make eighty-two different types of bread. Of these, **pita** (pee-tah) is the most popular. It is a round, flattish bread measuring about 10 inches (25.40cm) in diameter. It is made from either white or wheat flour.

Pita bread is the most popular type of Egyptian bread and is bought fresh daily by most citizens.

Bakeries all over Egypt bake fresh pita bread in huge brick ovens, similar to pizza ovens, every afternoon. The delicious aroma draws Egyptians who buy fresh pita bread everyday.

As the bread bakes, it puffs up and develops a soft crust. As it cools, it falls forming a pocket perfect for filling. Egyptians do just that, filling the bread with anything and everything. But they never overstuff it because they do not want the filling to overwhelm the yummy taste of the bread. Author Sally Elias Hanna explains: "Bread is so important to Egyptians that they prefer not to load the pita with too much meat or cheese. In fact, one slice of meat is about enough…. Egyptians like to taste their bread."[1]

Indeed, pita does not have to be filled for Egyptians to enjoy it. Many Egyptians do not use forks and spoons. For them, pita is not only a delicious food—it is their utensil. They use the bread to scoop up food and to sop up gravies.

Not Just Bread

As important as bread is, it is not the only way Egyptians use wheat. They use **bulgur**, wheat grain that has been hulled, steamed, and ground, in almost everything. Huge bins filled with bulgur are a common sight in markets throughout Egypt. The grain is sold in different grades, depending on its coarseness.

The wheat, which is soaked for at least two hours to make it tender before it is used, is put in soups, stews, casseroles, and salads. It is formed into ovals, stuffed

Wheat is the main ingredient in tabbouleh, a popular Egyptian salad that also contains tomatoes, parsley, and garlic.

with meat, and deep-fried to create a popular dish known as kobebeh (ko-beh-beh). Wheat is the main ingredient in **tabbouleh** (tah-boo-leh), a wheat, tomatoes, parsley, and garlic salad that is a mainstay of the Egyptian people's diet. It is, according to author Faye Levy, "fresh, colorful, satisfying and healthful too."[2]

Legumes

Legumes such as beans, peas, and lentils are another colorful and healthful part of the Egyptian diet. Egyptians have been eating them on a daily basis for thousands of years. Fava beans, chickpeas, and lentils are among the most popular. Egyptians eat them for breakfast, lunch, supper, and snacks. In fact, most Egyptians start their day with a bowl of fava beans, a practice that dates back to the time of the pharaohs. And, **bissara** (beh-sah-ra), a dip made of mashed fava beans, fried onions, mint, and spices accompanies many meals.

Red or yellow lentil soup served with pita bread and a slice of lemon is another ancient favorite. A 1200 B.C. fresco depicts cooks preparing it.

Hummus (hum-mus), a creamy dip made from chickpeas, lemon juice, garlic, and **tahini** (ta-hee-nee), which is a creamy sesame seed paste, is possibly the most well-known of all Middle Eastern recipes. Egyptians use pita bread to scoop up this tangy spread at meals and for snacks. It is, according to Tour Egypt on-line magazine, "One of the most common and most delicious dishes to be found in Egypt."[3]

Legumes, such as the three varieties pictured here, have been a staple of the Egyptian diet for thousands of years and can be eaten for all three meals.

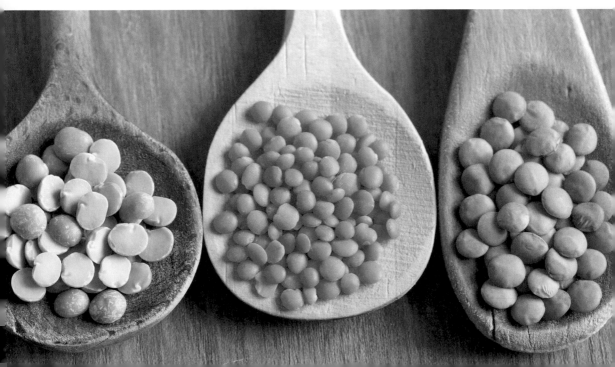

Lentil Soup

Egyptian lentil soup is usually made with red or yellow lentils. Gray lentils, which are readily available in the United States, can be substituted. This hearty soup can be a meal in itself.

Ingredients
1 cup lentils
1 carrot, sliced into small rounds
1 small onion, chopped
1 tomato, cut into chunks
1 can (16 oz.) chicken broth
½ teaspoon olive oil
½ teaspoon chopped parsley
pinch of cumin
pinch of salt

Instructions
1. Wash the lentils. Put them in a pot and cover them with water. Add onions, carrots, tomato, and salt and bring the mixture to a boil. Lower the heat and simmer the mixture for about 30–40 minutes, until the lentils and vegetables are tender.
2. Strain the mixture, then put it in a blender and puree.
3. Return the pureed mix to the pot, add the broth, oil, and cumin, and simmer for about 10 minutes. Sprinkle parsley on the soup before serving.

Serve with pita bread cut into quarters.
Serves 4.

Due to the hearty nature of lentil soup, it can be served as a meal.

Egyptians, as well as other Middle Eastern cultures, often use pita bread to scoop up hummus dip, which can be eaten as an appetizer or a snack.

More Valuable than Jewels

Dishes like hummus, bissara, and lentil soup would not taste or smell the same without the addition of spices. They give Egyptian cooking its irresistible aroma and unique flavor, transforming otherwise rustic dishes into works of arts.

In ancient times, Egypt was the center of the spice trade, which brought spices from India to the Middle East. At that time, spices were considered more valuable than jewels and were often used in place of money.

Modern Egyptians still value spices. More than two hundred different spices are sold in local bazaars or markets where they are sculpted into colorful pyramids and displayed in large and small baskets.

Hummus

Hummus is not difficult to make. Tahini is available in the international section of most supermarkets. Add more or less garlic, salt, and paprika to suit your taste.

Ingredients
1 can (16 oz.) chickpeas, drained
⅛ cup water
¼ cup tahini
⅛ cup lemon or lime juice
2 teaspoons olive oil
½ teaspoon garlic
½ teaspoon fresh chopped parsley
pinch of salt
pinch of paprika

Instructions
1. Put the chickpeas and water in a food processor or blender. Puree until the mixture is smooth.
2. Add the tahini, salt, garlic, and lemon juice and puree again. The mixture should be about as thick as yogurt. Add more water if necessary.
3. Transfer the mixture to a bowl. Press a spoon into the middle of the hummus to make a small well. Pour the olive oil into the well. Top with paprika and parsley.

Serve with pita bread.
Serves 2–4.

Tahini

Tahini (ta-HEE-nee) is made from sesame seeds that have been ground into a paste, forming a spread similar to peanut butter. Egyptians use tahini in many ways. Besides using it in hummus, they eat it alone, or they mix it with a little garlic and lemon juice as a savory dip for pita bread. It also serves as a popular salad dressing and a fish sauce. It is almost always served with kabobs, a favorite grilled meat dish, as well as being an important ingredient in Egyptian desserts. In many respects, tahini is the Egyptian equivalent of mayonnaise, but it is much healthier. It contains less fat and cholesterol, and more iron.

Like mayonnaise, tahini is a very versatile spread, but it is much healthier since it contains less fat and cholesterol.

Most Egyptian cooks do not like their food to taste fiery, nor do they like the taste of any one spice to dominate a dish. They use spices to flavor and perfume their cooking. With thousands of years of experience, they are experts at combining different spices in a way that enhances food's natural flavors. **Dukkah** (duh-kah) and **buharat** (buh-ha-raht) are two popular spice mixes. Dukkah is made with peanuts, sesame, cumin, and coriander seeds, which are ground into a fine powder. It is mixed with olive oil, and used in place of butter on pita bread. Buharat combines cinnamon, nutmeg, cumin, peppercorns, and cloves to create a sweet and savory spice mix that is used to season meat and fish.

When modern Egyptians flavor fish with spices, dip pita bread in dukkah, or eat a bowl of fava beans, it is almost as if they are reliving the past. Egyptian history is preserved in the food Egyptians eat. The herbs, legumes, and grains that Egyptians use today are the same ingredients that they relied on in ancient times. These staples give Egyptian cooking its characteristic fragrance and earthiness. It is no wonder these ingredients have withstood the test of time.

Healthy and Satisfying Meals

Egyptians' favorite dishes are nutritious and satisfying. Dishes like **ful medames** (fool mah-dahm-ees), salad, **moloukheyah** (mol-oh-hee-a), and **mahshi** (mah-shee) not only taste good, but they are loaded with essential nutrients.

The National Dish

Egypt is said to have two national dishes. Ful medames is one of them. It is a creamy fava bean dish that almost all Egyptians eat at least once a day. It is, according to author Jessica Harris, "consumed in the mansions of the rich and the huts of the poor."[4]

Ful medames is popular for breakfast, supper, and midnight snacks and has been for five thousand years.

Every Egyptian cook has his or her own recipe for the dish. There are probably as many variations as there are cooks in Egypt. But every cook starts the dish in the same way. They slowly simmer fava beans flavored with lemon juice, olive oil, and any number of spices overnight.

By morning, the beans are soft and moist. In the past, the beans were cooked in large metal pots with narrow necks that were buried in hot embers overnight. The shape of the pot kept the beans hot while allowing some steam to escape through the narrow top. Today the beans are more likely to be cooked on a stovetop in an ordinary pot, but the taste remains the same.

When the beans are done, they are mashed to a creamy consistency similar to refried beans. They are topped with a fried or hard-boiled egg and a sprinkle of parsley. Hot toasted pita bread and pickled vegetables are served on the side.

Special bean eateries all over Egypt sell the delicious dish. Lines to purchase the meal start forming early in the morning and continue well into the night. Egyptian native Hassan El-Foly explains that ful medames is

Ful Medames

This is a quick and easy way to make ful me-dames. It uses canned fava beans, which also are called broad beans. If you prefer to use dried beans, you should soak the beans overnight, then cook them for about two hours. If you cannot find fava beans, any pink bean can be substituted.

Ingredients
1 16-oz. can fava (broad) beans, undrained
2 tablespoons lemon juice
⅛ cup olive oil
1 teaspoon garlic powder
salt and pepper to taste
1 tablespoon chopped parsley
2 peeled hard boiled eggs (optional)
2 chopped green onions (optional)

Instructions
1. Put fava beans along with their liquid into a small pot. Bring to a boil over medium heat.
2. Reduce the heat. Simmer for five minutes.
3. Put the beans in a large bowl. Use a fork to mash the beans into a paste.
4. Mix the olive oil, garlic powder, lemon juice, and salt and pepper. Pour the mix on the beans, then stir. Top with parsley.
Offer green onions and eggs on the side. Serve with pita bread.
Serves 2.

"popular because it has high protein and it will fill you up with all the energy you need for the day."[5]

The delicious dish is extremely nourishing. Not only is it loaded with protein, it is an excellent source of fiber, complex carbohydrates, and B vitamins. Fava beans also contain natural substances that cause the brain to release chemicals, which impart feelings of calmness and well-being. It is no wonder that ful medames is so popular.

Green Soup

Moloukheyah also is very popular, and is Egypt's other national dish. This dark green soup is made from mallow, a native green similar to spinach. Egyptians have been growing mallow in planters around their homes

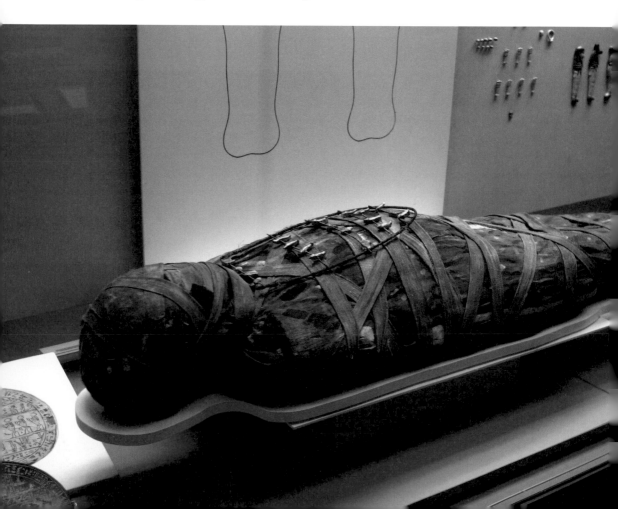

and turning their harvest into moloukheyah for thousands of years. In fact, the growing of mallow and the making of the soup is depicted on ancient tomb murals. By using DNA tests, scientists have even discovered remains of the soup in the stomachs of mummies.

Moloukheyah is made by chopping and rechopping mallow leaves until a paste forms. The leaves, which are naturally sticky, are then cooked in a flavorful meat or chicken broth seasoned with cardamom and coriander. When the soup is almost done, fried garlic is added to the pot. The rich and spicy aroma is amazing.

The soup is often served over a mound of rice, pieces of meat, and/or chunks of pita bread. Lemon slices accompany it. It has a hearty taste and a stringy texture that Egyptians adore. They like the dish so much that in 399 A.D. when an Egyptian ruler banned the soup because his enemy loved it, many Egyptians risked flogging, or beatings, just to eat it.

Like ful medames, moloukheyah is very nourishing. It is low in calories and fat, and high in protein, fiber, calcium, iron, and vitamins A and B. But that is not the only reason Egyptians cannot get enough of the rich soup. They adore the soup's taste. Egyptians, according to Cairo resident John Feeny, "find the very name mulukhiyah [moloukheyah] mouth watering."[6]

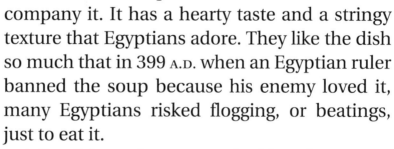

Egyptians have been making moloukheyah, or green soup, for so long that remains of the soup have been found in the stomachs of mummies, like the one pictured here.

Stuffed Leaves and Vegetables

Mahshi, stuffed leaves and vegetables, is another Egyptian specialty. Egypt has always produced a wide variety of vegetables and edible leaves. Artichokes, eggplants, cabbage, squash, and grape leaves are national favorites. Egyptians like to fill these vegetables with some combination of rice, meat, onions, tomatoes, mint, and spices.

Ground lamb is the most common meat used. Egyptians have raised sheep since ancient time, and lamb is the most popular meat in Egypt. Beef is more expensive than lamb, and pork is rarely eaten. Most Egyptians are Muslims, and their religion forbids the eating of pork.

Any vegetable can be stuffed. Stuffed grape leaves filled with onions, rice, ground meat, and spices are extremely popular. Egyptians harvest young grape leaves in the spring, when they are fresh and sweet. They boil the leaves to make them easy to work with. Then, they lay the leaves down flat and place a spoonful of the filling at the bottom of each leaf. They fold the bottom and two sides of the leaf over the filling and carefully roll the leaf tip to form a tube shape. The stuffed leaves are slowly simmered in a rich meat broth until they are fork-tender.

Artichokes stuffed with ground meat and simmered in tomato sauce also are a favorite dish. Slender black and white eggplants filled with a mixture of rice, meat, mint, and parsley also are enjoyed by Egyptians.

Vegetables stuffed in this manner are a meal in

Although any vegetable can be stuffed with rice, meats, and spices, stuffed grape leaves are probably the most popular with Egyptians.

Shopping in Egypt

Egypt has many modern supermarket chains that carry a wide range of foods. There also are an abundance of little grocery stores. On the coast, fish markets sell freshly caught fish. Some fish markets also cook and serve fish to order. Bakeries, which are actually just open stands, offer freshly baked bread.

There also are large outdoor markets or bazaars. Such markets are often set in a maze of small streets and alleys where vendors in small stores and stalls called *souks* sell anything and everything. Shoppers can buy jewelry, smoking accessories, books, clothing, leather goods, glassware, live animals, fresh fruit and vegetables, and spices, to name a few items. Some of these bazaars are quite old. The one in Cairo dates back to the 1400s.

This outdoor bazaar in Cairo, Egypt, dates back to the 1400s and sells everything from food to clothing and jewelry.

themselves. They are satisfying, delectable, and loaded with nutrients. "Stuffed vegetables are a huge favorite among Egyptians," author Magda Mehdawy explains, "since they contain a relatively high level of vitamins and minerals they are essential for good health, as well as rice, which is a carbohydrate, and ground meat, which is a rich source of protein."[7]

Fresh Salad

Egyptians not only eat vegetables and leaves cooked and stuffed, they adore them in salads. No matter the main dish, a salad loaded with fresh healthy vegetables and herbs accompanies almost every Egyptian meal. According to author Anissa Helou, "Salads are a main-

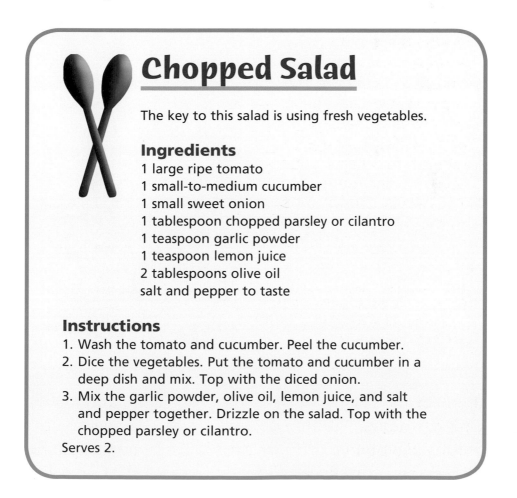

Chopped Salad

The key to this salad is using fresh vegetables.

Ingredients
1 large ripe tomato
1 small-to-medium cucumber
1 small sweet onion
1 tablespoon chopped parsley or cilantro
1 teaspoon garlic powder
1 teaspoon lemon juice
2 tablespoons olive oil
salt and pepper to taste

Instructions
1. Wash the tomato and cucumber. Peel the cucumber.
2. Dice the vegetables. Put the tomato and cucumber in a deep dish and mix. Top with the diced onion.
3. Mix the garlic powder, olive oil, lemon juice, and salt and pepper together. Drizzle on the salad. Top with the chopped parsley or cilantro.
Serves 2.

Egyptians insist that only the freshest vegetables be used in their salads, like the chopped salad pictured here.

stay…and traditional meals always include at least one, more often two or three. Many are packed with fresh herbs such as parsley (full of iron) and mint (full of antioxidants) and eating a plateful…is like having an instant shot of good health."[8]

There are myriad of different salads to choose from. A chopped salad is probably the most popular. It is made with a colorful mix of tomatoes, onions, and cucumbers, dressed with olive oil, lemon juice, garlic, and a sprinkle of fresh herbs like parsley or cilantro.

Not just any vegetables will do. Many Egyptians are fanatical about the quality of their vegetables. They insist on only the freshest, juiciest vegetables for their salads. Most are fresh off the vine. In fact, street vendors sell farm fresh tomatoes loaded with juice door-to-door throughout Egypt.

The cucumbers are special too. These local treasures are smaller and thinner than those grown in the United States and have a sweet flavor. "Everyone knows that the quality of the tomatoes is of great importance," Levy explains. "But this is also true of the cucumber…. These are small, thin cucumbers. They are crisp, delicately sweet, and have tender skin with no trace of bitterness."[9]

Although the salad is quite simple, the freshness and quality of the vegetables give it a juicy brightness that is hard to resist. "All around the region people love it,"[10] says Levy.

Indeed, Egyptian cooks have managed to marry good taste with nutrition in their favorite dishes. Chopped salad, ful medames, molokheya, and stuffed vegetables are all extraordinarily delicious and healthy. It is not surprising that Egyptians love them.

Chapter 3

Irresistible Street Food

Egyptian street food is world famous. Brightly painted carts, street stalls, and tiny cafés are everywhere. Tempted by the mouth-watering aromas, hungry passersby often stop to sample one delicacy after another, including the popular favorites **koshari** (ko-shah-ree), **falafel** (feh-lah-fil), **kebabs** (ke-baabs), **shawarma** (shah-wahr-mah), and **kofta** (kof-tah).

An Ancient Fast Food

Koshari may be the world's oldest fast food. It dates back more than one thousand years. It is a hearty dish made with pasta, rice, lentils, fried onions, garlic, and spices. Vendors working from wheeled carts, or in fast food restaurants that sell nothing but koshari, stand in front of an array of large cooking pots each containing a different ingredient. After a customer places an order, the vendor, who is traditionally a man, layers each ingredient into an aluminum bowl. As he switches ingredients, he bangs his spoon on the side of the bowl

Egyptian Pizza

Fiteer (fi-teer) is a favorite Egyptian snack food. It is often described as "Egyptian pizza," because like pizza dough, fiteer dough is tossed into the air to stretch it. But there is a difference. Pizza dough is stretched into a one-layer disc. Fiteer dough is stretched and then folded to form layers. The result is a light, flaky bread.

Egyptians eat fiteer spread with oil, butter, jam, or wild honey. They also eat it stuffed with a variety of fillings including a combination of ground meat, egg, and tomato, or mushrooms and cheese.

Fiteer is sometimes described as "Egyptian pizza" because its dough is tossed into the air to be stretched similar to the way pizza dough is stretched.

Koshari is an Egyptian dish in which the cook layers different ingredients in an aluminum bowl. It is considered the original Egyptian fast food since most koshari cooks can make an order in about five seconds.

to clean it off before adding the next layer. It sounds as if he is drumming, but Egyptians do not mind the noise. Wael Fawaz, a Syrian student studying in Cairo, explains: "The restaurants of koshary [koshari] are very noisy. One sits to eat while the koshary man practices his drums in your ears. It's weird but I guess it's part of the Egyptian identity, which you get use[d] to in time."[11]

Koshari eateries are usually mobbed; but the line moves fast. Good koshari cooks can prepare an order in

Camel Meat

Egyptians have always eaten kamaal or camel meat. It is a red meat that tastes similar to beef. It is virtually fat-free because camels store their fat in their humps.

Camels that are raised for meat are slaughtered when they are between two and four years old. After this, the meat becomes too tough to eat. Camel meat often is ground and mixed with rice to make meat-balls.

The meat also is rubbed with spices and boiled. It takes three to four hours to cook this way. Egyptians eat the broth that forms when they boil the meat. The broth is colorless and fat-free. They add tomato juice and fat cut from the camel's hump to the broth to give it color and flavor.

These camels are being transported to slaughter in Cairo. Camel meat has always been eaten in Egypt.

five seconds, which gives new meaning to the term fast food. Aziz Awad, a Cairo koshari vendor explains: "I have to be fast. My hands are accustomed to the same movements I do all day everyday, so you can say that I memorized the movements rather than think about

Kofta

Kofta can be made with any kind of ground meat. This recipes uses ground beef. You can make kofta in a frying pan or grill it on skewers on a grill or in a broiler.

Ingredients
1 lb. ground beef
1 small onion, chopped
1 tablespoon chopped parsley
½ teaspoon cumin
½ teaspoon coriander
salt and pepper to taste

Instructions
1. Mix all the ingredients together. Form a handful of the meat mixture into a meatball. Put three or four meatballs on each skewer. Leave space on the top and bottom of the skewer. Press the meatballs together to form a cigar shape.
2. Grill the meat on a grill or in a broiler. Let the meat brown on one side, then turn the skewers over. The meat is done when it is brown on both sides.
3. Remove the meat from the skewers.

Serve with pita bread and yogurt salad.
Serves 4.

Kofta is a very versatile recipe since it can use any type of meat and can be either fried, grilled, or broiled.

them."[12]

Egyptians eat koshari as a snack or as a quick meal. They top it with hot chili sauce, which adds a spicy zing. The result is layer upon layer of hearty flavors that stick to the ribs for hours. "Koshary is something I love," says Waleed Abdullah, an Egyptian office worker. "I can have it…anytime, anywhere. I can eat it standing, sitting, at work or at home. It's…both affordable and delicious."[13]

Skewered Meats

Meat grilled on a spit over a charcoal fire is another Egyptian favorite. The Ottomans or Turks brought this style of cooking to Egypt in the sixteenth century when they occupied Egypt. Kebabs, shawarma, and kofta are popular choices.

Kebabs are chunks of lamb or beef, which have been marinated, or soaked, overnight in a mixture of spices, olive oil, lemon juice, or yogurt. The acid in the marinating liquid makes the already tender meat as soft as butter.

When the meat is ready for cooking, it is threaded onto a skewer between chunks of onion and pepper. The skewer is turned, and the meat is brushed with still more marinade as it cooks. When the meat is brown on the outside and juicy on the inside, and the vegetables are soft and sweet, the meat and vegetables are removed from the skewer and put on a plate along with salad and warm pita bread. Egyptians use the bread to scoop up the meat and sop up the savory juices.

Although an Egyptian favorite, kebabs were actually a style of cooking brought to Egypt by the Ottomans or Turks in the sixteenth century.

Yogurt Salad

Kofta and kebabs are often served with yogurt salad. Egyptian yogurt is unflavored, freshly made, and is thinner than American yogurt. The yogurt mix also makes a tasty party dip. It is simple to make and very healthy. You can add more salt, garlic, and black pepper to suit your taste.

Ingredients
1 cup plain yogurt
½ medium cucumber, peeled and cut in chunks
½ tablespoon garlic powder
pinch of salt
½ tablespoon dried mint

Instructions
1. Combine all the ingredients in a bowl. Mix well.
2. Refrigerate for at least one hour before serving.
Serves 4.

When Egyptians want the meat stuffed inside bread, they eat shawarma. It is probably the most popular sandwich in Egypt. Shawarma is made of large round slices of marinated lamb layered one on top of another on a long vertical skewer. A slice of fat is placed between every few layers. As the meat grills, the fat drips and moistens the meat making it pull-apart tender and forming a crispy outer crust.

While it is cooking, shawarma looks like a giant meat cylinder. Vendors cut thin slices of the meat and stuff them into pita bread with some salad and tahini.

People all over Egypt, "grab these hot satisfying sandwiches on the run,"[14] according to Levy.

Kofta is another popular grilled meat choice. It is the Egyptian version of a hamburger. Instead of slices or chunks of meat, it is made of ground lamb mixed with chopped onion and spices. The meat is rolled around a skewer in a sausage shape and grilled until it is hot and juicy. Kofta is usually accompanied by a tangy yogurt salad made of sliced cucumber, dressed with freshly made yogurt, garlic, and mint.

Between kofta, shawarma, and kebabs, Egyptians have many grilled dishes to choose from. That is a good thing because, as Egyptian journalist Ali El Bahnasawy says: "Egyptians love their grilled meats."[15]

Fried Bean Patties

Egyptians also love falafel. It is a carefully seasoned fried bean patty, which also is known as taamiya (ta-mi-yah) in Egypt. Falafel is popular throughout the Middle East. It is made with chickpeas in most other countries, but not in Egypt. Here, fava beans are used.

To make falafel, cooks mash the beans with fresh herbs such as dill, parsley, cilantro, coriander, and garlic. Next, the cook forms the mixture into patties with a tool similar to an ice cream scoop. The little cakes are fried in oil that is neither too hot nor too cool. The oil temperature is important because if it is too cool the felafel will taste soggy. If it is too hot, the crust will get too crunchy.

Frying only takes a few seconds. The spicy bean

cakes are done when they are crisp and golden on the outside and soft on the inside. Because of the herbs, the inside has a greenish tint. "Biting into the crisp brown crust," explains John Feeny, "reveals a heart that is bright green from all those leaves."[16]

Falafel is topped with sesame seeds and served with

pita bread, chopped salad, pickled vegetables, and tahini, which moistens the bean cake. It is available all over Egypt. It is sold in fast food chains like McDonalds, which offers McFalafel sandwiches, in special eateries that sell nothing but falafel, in upscale restaurants, and by street vendors who push brightly colored carts. The shape and design of these carts vary according to the food sold. "Falafel carts are long and red, and have a wide ledge, on one side of which is the falafel fryer and, on the other, a mound of pita bread. In between are large bowls piled high with different garnishes such as pickles, chopped salad, and chips, plus a jug of tahini sauce," explains Anissa Helou. "The gas bottle, which feeds the burner under the falafel frying pan is kept by the side of the cart. The panels are covered with Arabic writing, suras [sayings] from the Quran [the Islamic holy book], the vendor's name and various superlatives [exaggerated descriptions] telling you why you should

Irresistible Street Food

eat at the vendor's stall…. I can never resist stopping at an Egyptian falafel vendor's cart."[17]

Egyptian streets are clearly a snacker's paradise. The tantalizing aroma of juicy meat grilling on a spit, koshari bubbling in large vats, and herb-scented falafel frying in hot oil fill the air. It is no wonder that Egyptian street food is famous, or that Egyptians find these foods hard to resist.

Chapter 4

A Time for Sharing

Most Egyptian celebrations are tied to Muslim holy days. **Ramadan** (Rah-mah-dahn), a month-long religious holiday that falls at different times each year, is the most joyous time of the year. Egyptians commemorate it by sharing special foods with each other.

Ramadan Fast and Feast

Ramadan is celebrated with as much happiness and excitement in Egypt as Christmas is in the United States. During Ramadan, Muslims typically fast from dawn to dusk in an effort to purify their souls. This means that they limit food and drink. Daily meals are reduced to two: *sohour* (so-hoor), a pre-dawn meal that starts the daily fast, and *iftar* (if-tahr), the evening meal that

A Special Day

Ramadan begins at the start of the ninth month of the Islamic calendar and ends on the last day of the month. Eid al-Fitr is a holiday celebrating the end of Ramadan. It is held on the first three days of the month following Ramadan. During Eid, Egyptian children receive gifts of new clothes and money. Egyptian women also are given gifts by their loved ones. Families get together on this holiday. Roads and train stations are very busy.

Once family members have gathered, many take felucca rides on the Nile River. Feluccas are traditional wooden sailing boats used in Egypt. Many go to parks, zoos, or botanical gardens where they have picnics.

Kahk, cookies made with spices, sesame seeds, ground black cherry pits, and walnuts, and dusted with sugar are always eaten during Eid. Bakeries start selling the cookies on the last few days of Ramadan.

A felucca boat sailing on the Nile River during Ramadan. Felucca rides are just one tradition that Egyptians follow during Ramadan.

breaks it. Egyptians eat liberally at both meals. In fact, they consider it rude not to eat everything on their plates.

Iftar, in particular, is a rich meal at which it is customary to share special foods with family, friends, and neighbors. No one is supposed to eat iftar alone. Even strangers are invited to the iftar feast. For those who are too poor to buy food for their families, local merchants donate food for charity meals that are served on Egyptian streets. Cairo journalist Amira Pierce describes a typical scene: "Down streets and alleyways, people from the neighborhood sit at long tables, each in front of a piece of bread and a date waiting for sunset to be official. These are charity meals, provided by

A charity meal being served in an Egyptian street during Ramadan.

Stuffed Dates

Stuffed dates are easy to make. You also can stuff prunes in the same way. Pecans can be substituted for walnuts. The stuffed dates can be rolled in sugar instead of coconut, depending on your taste.

Ingredients
12 pitted dates
12 walnut halves, shelled
1 cup shredded coconut

Instructions
1. Put the shredded coconut in a shallow bowl.
2. Make a slit in the center of each date.
3. Stuff a walnut half into the slit.
4. Roll the dates in coconut until they are covered.

Makes 12 stuffed dates.

Stuffed dates are a favorite Egyptian treat and are easy to make.

a neighborhood benefactor [supporter] to anyone, no questions asked each night of Ramadan."[18] Iftar menus vary, but it is customary to start the feast with dates, a tradition that began in the seventh century when Islam's prophet Mohammed broke his daily fast with the sweet fruit.

Dates grow well in Egypt's hot climate and have been a staple here since ancient times. During Ramadan, vendors sell dates from street stalls all over Egypt. The sweet fruits are often stuffed. To do this, cooks remove the seed from the middle of the date and replace it with a walnut half. Then, they roll the date in shredded coconut. The result is naturally sweet, pleasantly crunchy, and deliciously fragrant.

Cooked Pigeon

Dates are usually followed by soup and a celebratory main course. This course may feature lamb, poultry, fish, or legumes. **Hamam** (Ham-aam), or stuffed pigeon, is a popular favorite.

Egyptians have been raising pigeons for food for thousands of years. Even the pharaohs ate the little birds. These birds are not the same birds that are seen in parks and city streets. These birds are specially bred for food. "I pick them live at the market twice a week," explains Cairo chef Mahmoud Amin Farahat. "I feel them for their plumpness and check their health."[19]

Rooftop pigeon coops are a common sight in Egyptian cities, and pigeon towers dot the countryside. These tall structures are shaped like rocket ships with dozens of holes made of mud. The holes improve the airflow in the towers, which helps keep the pigeons

Pigeon towers, like the one pictured here, can be seen all over the Egyptian countryside. It is in these towers that pigeons are raised to be used for hamam, or stuffed pigeon, a popular Egyptian dish.

healthy. "Almost every farmhouse has its own pigeon tower made of Nile mud," Feeny explains. "In some parts of the Delta there are veritable pigeon cities—lofty skyscraper complexes housing tens of thousands of pigeons—for pigeons are also raised commercially and served in the most sophisticated restaurants as well as the most humble homes."[20]

Pigeons bred for food are slaughtered before they are old enough to fly, which ensures that the meat is tender. Cooks stuff the pigeons with rice seasoned with cinnamon, or with **fireek** (freek), coarsely crushed wheat grain that is harvested when it is still green, mixed with onions, garlic, mint, and butter. Sometimes, the cooks bury the pigeon's head in the stuffing. Although this might not appeal to Western taste, for Egyptians, finding the head is like discovering a hidden treasure.

Edible Bracelets

Almond rings, which look like women's bracelets, are a special treat that are often served at wedding showers and engagement parties in Egypt. The pastries are made from ground almonds, sugar, egg whites, and orange blossom water, a fragrant mixture made with orange blossoms and water.

The dough is rolled into a sausage shape and the ends are brought together to form a ring. The "bracelets" are about the size of a napkin ring. They are a little too small to fit on most brides' wrists. Sometimes "jewels" in the form of whole almonds are pressed into the dough to adorn it.

Basboosa

This recipe calls for semolina flour. Cream of wheat cereal (which has a 2 1/2 minute cooking time) can be substituted. For something different, try basboosa with a scoop of vanilla ice cream on top.

Ingredients

For the basboosa:
2 cups semolina flour
1 cup plain yogurt
1 cup butter or margarine, melted
½ cup sugar
1 cup shredded coconut flakes
2 eggs, beaten
1 ½ teaspoons baking powder
1 teaspoon vanilla
blanched almonds

For the syrup:
1 cup water
1 cup sugar
1 tablespoon butter
2 teaspoons lemon juice

Instructions

1. Preheat the oven to 350 degrees.
2. For the basboosa combine the flour, sugar, coconut, and baking powder in a bowl.
3. Add the eggs, butter, yogurt, and vanilla and mix well.
4. Grease an 11 x 7 inch (28 x18cm) baking pan and pour in the mixture.
5. Decorate with the almonds.
6. Bake in the oven for about 30 minutes or until the basboosa is golden and a fork poked into the middle comes out clean.
7. Take the basboosa out of the oven and cool.
8. While the basboosa is baking, combine the sugar, water, and lemon juice in a saucepan and boil, stirring so the sugar dissolves. Add the butter and remove from the heat.
9. Pour the syrup over the basboosa. Let the syrup cool completely. Then cut the basboosa into small squares.

Makes about 18 squares.

 Foods of Egypt

Once the bird is stuffed, it is coated with spices and grilled or roasted until it is crispy on the outside and moist and succulent within. Hamam often is served on a nest of lettuce leaves and alfalfa sprouts. A mound of hot fluffy pita bread, chopped salad, tahini, pickled vegetables, and a creamy garlic lemon sauce accompany it. The results, according to celebrated world traveler Anthony Bourdain, are "utterly delicious."[21]

Sweet Gifts

After eating dates, soup, a main course like hamam, salad, and bread, most diners are stuffed by the time dessert arrives. But the feast is not over until sweets, symbolizing the joy and sweetness of Ramadan, are served. Presenting the iftar host and hostess with a sweet treat is an Egyptian custom, and iftar guests never arrive empty-handed. It is not uncommon for the iftar table to be piled high with these sweet gifts.

Bakeries and street stalls all over Egypt offer a huge array of Ramadan sweets. Enticing aromas drift from these shops, tempting iftar guests to purchase their favorites. Among these are **yameesh** (yah-meesh), **konafa** (co-nah-fuh), **qatayef** (kah-tah-yef), and **basboosa** (bas-boo-sah).

Yameesh is the simplest of these treats. It is a mix of dried fruit and nuts. Delicacies like figs, raisins, prunes, dried apricots, almonds, walnuts, hazelnuts, and pistachio nuts are prettily displayed on a platter forming a colorful arrangement that is as pleasing to the eyes as to the taste buds.

Konafa is just one of the freshly baked desserts served during Ramadan by Egyptians.

Qatayef, too, is pretty to look at, but it is this pastry's fragrance that makes it extra special. It is perfumed with rosewater, a liquid made with distilled water and rose petals. The scent is delicate and exotic, and so is the taste. Qatayef is similar to a pancake. It is made by frying sweet batter on a griddle. When one side is done, the pancake is removed from the griddle and then filled with a mixture of ground nuts and spices, or sweet cheese. The thick fluffy pancake is folded into a half moon and sealed by pressing the edges. It is then fried or baked. When the delicacy is golden brown, it is topped with syrup made with sugar or honey, and rosewater.

Qatayef is made only during Ramadan. Women, known as qatayef ladies, set up carts and stalls all over Egypt. Long lines of holiday celebrants crowd these stalls.

Egyptians also mob bakeries and stands that sell

freshly baked basboosa and konafa. Basbossa are thin pastry squares made from grains of ground wheat called semolina. It also contains shredded coconut, sugar, yogurt, and lots of butter. An almond is placed in the center of each square, and hot fragrant syrup is poured over it. Basbossa is extremely sweet. One little square satisfies even the most demanding sweet tooth.

Konafa, too, is topped with hot syrup. Making this pastry is an art. This crisp golden delicacy begins with thread-like strips of sweet flaky dough. To get the dough thin enough, the kanafani, or konafa baker, puts it through a metal funnel equipped with a fine sieve, or strainer. As the dough passes through the sieve, pale yellow dough threads, so thin that they are almost invisible, form. The threads are placed in a baking pan and topped with almonds, raisins, and spices, or fresh sweet cream, then covered with still more threads.

Konafa is traditionally fried on a hot grill, although it also can be baked. When it is done, the stringy dough looks like shredded wheat. Hot syrup is poured on top. The syrup caramelizes as the dessert cools. Konafa tastes soft, sweet, buttery, and crunchy all at the same time. "I could not believe the taste,"[22] says Sharmi, an Indian cook who recently tried the dessert.

Delicious foods like konafa seem to taste even better when they are shared. "That's what Ramadan is all about: sharing,"[23] explains Egyptian journalist Noha Mohammed. Getting together with loved ones and sharing food is one of the joys of Ramadan. Special dishes and sweet desserts add to the delight of the season.

Mass (weight)

1 ounce (oz.)	= 28.0 grams (g)
8 ounces	= 227.0 grams
1 pound (lb.) or 16 ounces	= 0.45 kilograms (kg)
2.2 pounds	= 1.0 kilogram

Liquid Volume

1 teaspoon (tsp.)	= 5.0 milliliters (ml)
1 tablespoon (tbsp.)	= 15.0 milliliters
1 fluid ounce (oz.)	= 30.0 milliliters
1 cup (c.)	= 240 milliliters
1 pint (pt.)	= 480 milliliters
1 quart (qt.)	= 0.96 liters (l)
1 gallon (gal.)	= 3.84 liters

Pan Sizes

8- inch cake pan	= 20 x 4-centimeter cake pan
9-inch cake pan	= 23 x 3.5-centimeter cake pan
11 x 7-inch baking pan	= 28 x 18-centimeter baking pan
13 x 9-inch baking pan	= 32.5 x 23-centimeter baking pan
9 x 5-inch loaf pan	= 23 x 13-centimeter loaf pan
2-quart casserole	= 2-liter casserole

Temperature

212°F	= 100°C (boiling point of water)
225°F	= 110°C
250°F	= 120°C
275°F	= 135°C
300°F	= 150°C
325°F	= 160°C
350°F	= 180°C
375°F	= 190°C
400°F	= 200°C

Length

1/4 inch (in.)	= 0.6 centimeters (cm)
1/2 inch	= 1.25 centimeters
1 inch	= 2.5 centimeters

Notes

Chapter 1: Ancient Ingredients

1. Sally Elias Hanna, *Dining on the Nile*, Indianapolis: Dog Ear Publishing, 2006, p. 41.

2. Faye Levy, Feast from the Mideast, New York: Harper Collins, 2003, p. 77.

3. Mary Kay Radnick, "Behold the Power of the Chickpea," *Tour Egypt Monthly*, August 1, 2000. http://www.touregypt.net/magazine/mag08012000/mag5.htm.

Chapter 2: Healthy and Satisfying Meals

4. Jessica B. Harris, *The African Cookbook*, New York: Simon and Schuster, 1998, p. 204.

5. Quoted in Monica Eng, "Feasting on Favas," *Chicago Tribune.com*, September 27, 2006, http://archives.chicago tribune.com/2006/sep/27/food/chi-0609270022sep27

6. John Feeny, "The Good Things of Egypt," *Saudi Aramco World*, November/December 1975. http://www.saudiaramcoworld.com/issue/197506/the.good.things.of.egypt.htm.

7. Magda Mehdawy, *My Egyptian Grandmother's Kitchen*, Cairo: The American University in Cairo Press, 2006, p. 90.

8. Anissa Helou, "Food & Drink Bon Appétit," *Gulf Life*, November 1, 2008. http://www.gulf-life.com/2008/11/01/bon-appetit/.

9. Faye Levy, *Feast from the Mideast*, p. 59.

10. Faye Levy, *Feast from the Mideast*, p. 58.

Chapter 3: Irresistible Street Food

11. Quoted in Helen Fateen Bizzari, "Koshary," *Tour Egypt Monthly*, June 18, 2004. www.touregypt.net/featurestories/koshary.htm.

12. Quoted in Helen Fateen Bizzari, "Koshary." www.touregypt.net/featurestories/koshary.htm.

13. Quoted in Helen Fateen Bizzari, "Koshary." www.touregypt.net/featurestories/koshary.htm.

14. Faye Levy, *Feast from the Mideast*, p.196.

15. Ali El Bahnasawy, "Street Food Done Right," *Egypt Today*, January 2009. http://www.egypttoday.com/article.aspx?ArticleID=8320.

16. John Feeny, "The Good Things of Egypt," http://www.saudiaramcoworld.com/issue/197506/the.good.things.of.egypt.htm.

17. Anissa Helou, "Street Food," *Gulf Life*, January 1, 2008, www.gulf-life.com/2008/01/01/street-food-3/.

Chapter 4: A Time for Sharing

18. Amira Pierce, "Letters from Egypt: Ramadan and Firecrackers," The Morning News, November 4, 2004. http://www.themorningnews.org/archives/opinions/letters_from_egypt_ramadan_and_firecrackers.php.

19. Quoted in Daniel Williams, "Happiness is a Warm Pigeon in Old Egypt Bazaar: Cairo Dining," Bloomberg.com, March 27, 2007. http://www.bloomberg.com/apps/news?pid=20670001&sid=adma.1F9hF_o.

20. John Feeny, "The Good Things of Egypt," http://www.saudiaramcoworld.com/issue/197506/the.good.things.of.egypt.htm.

21. Anthony Bourdain, "No Reservations Egypt," The Travel Channel, August 2008.

22. Nievedyam, "Konafah-Arabian Nights Special!" March 27, 2007. http://www.neivedyam.com/2007/03/konafah-arabian-nights-special.html.

23. Noha Mohammed, "Counting Our Blessings," Egypt Today, September 2007. http://egypttoday.com/article.aspx?ArticleID=7673.

Glossary

aish: the Egyptian word for bread and life.

antioxidants: substances that strengthen the body by fighting against chemicals that cause disease.

basboosa: pastry made with semolina.

bissara: a dip made of mashed fava beans, fried onions, mint, and spices.

buharat: a spice mixture made with cinnamon, nutmeg, cumin, peppercorns, and cloves used to season meat and fish.

bulgur: hulled, steamed, and ground wheat grain.

dukkah: a spice mix made with peanuts, sesame, cumin, and coriander seeds, which are ground into a fine powder, or mixed with olive oil and spread on bread.

falafel: bean cakes.

fireek: coarsely crushed wheat grain that is harvested when it is still green.

ful medames: a fava bean dish.

hamam: pigeon dishes.

hummus: a dip made from chickpeas, lemon juice, and garlic.

iftar: a meal eaten after sunset when the daily Ramadan fast ends.

kebabs: grilled skewered meat chunks.

kofta: chopped meat wrapped around a skewer and grilled.

konafa: a sweet pastry made with thread-like strands of dough.

koshari: layers of pasta, lentils, and rice.

legumes: beans, peas, and lentils.

mahshi: edible leaves and vegetables stuffed with meat and rice.

moloukheyah: a soup made from mallow, a green similar to spinach.

pita: round, flat pocket bread.

qatayef: a pancake-like dessert.

Ramadan: a month-long religious holiday in which Muslims fast from dawn to dusk.

shawarma: layers of meat grilled on a skewer.

sohour: a pre-dawn meal eaten before the daily Ramadan fast begins.

taamiya: an Egyptian term for falafel.

tabbouleh: a wheat, tomatoes, parsley, and garlic salad.

tahini: a creamy sesame-seed paste.

yameesh: dried fruit and nuts.

For Further Exploration

Books

Alison Behnke, *Cooking the Middle Eastern Way*. Minneapolis: Lerner Publications, 2005. This is a cookbook for kids featuring recipes from various countries including Egypt.

Linda Honan, *Spend the Day in Ancient Egypt*. New York: John Wiley Inc., 1999. A simple book that details life in ancient Egypt. Craft activities and a few recipes are included.

Arlene Moscovitch, *Egypt: The People*. New York: Crabtree, 2008. How people live in modern Egypt is the theme of this book.

Don Nardo, *Daily Life: Ancient Egypt*. San Diego: KidHaven Press, 2002. This excellent book gives details about daily life in ancient Egypt.

Jeffrey Zuehike, *Egypt in Pictures*. Minneapolis: Lerner Publications, 2002. This book covers all aspects of Egyptian life including geography, history, government, religion, people, and culture. It has many photographs.

Web Sites

The British Museum, "Ancient Egypt." (http://www.ancientegypt.co.uk/menu.html). This museum Web site offers a wealth of information about life in ancient Egypt. It includes pictures, stories, and games.

People and Places, "Egypt: Some Basic Facts," *Kidcyber*. (www.kidcyber.com.au/topics/Egypt.htm). Information just for kids about Egypt including dozens of interesting and interactive links.

Tour Egypt, "Recipes." (http://touregypt.net/recipes/). Dozens of recipes are presented here.

Tour Egypt for Kids, "Color Me Egypt," *Tour Egypt*. (http://www.touregypt.net/kids/). This Web site gives kids lots of information about ancient and modern Egypt. It has a link to an Egyptian girl's blog, and activities, stories, and games.

Index

Picture credits

About the Author

Barbara Sheen is the author of more than fifty books for young people. She lives in New Mexico with her family. In her spare time, she likes to swim, walk, garden, and read. Of course, she loves to cook!